To _____

From _____

REFLECTING JESUS
TO
TINY TOTS

By
Peggy A. Kazebier

TEACH Services, Inc.
Brushton, New York

2008 09 10 11 12 · 5 4 3 2 1

Copyright © 2008 TEACH Services, Inc.
ISBN-13: 978-1-57258-495-2
ISBN-10: 1-57258-495-5
Library of Congress Control Number: 2008925609

Published by
TEACH Services, Inc.
www.TEACHServices.com

UNIVERSE

"...God created the heavens and the earth" (Genesis 1:1 NKJV).

When God said, "Let there be light," there was light. Each day He spoke for different things and they were there. But when He made man He carefully formed him from the dust of the ground, in His own image (Genesis 2:7, 1:26). That makes us very special!

Do you feel special? God made you. He loves you.

BABY JESUS

An angel said to the shepherds, "You will find a Babe...lying in a manger" (Luke 2:12 NKJV).

The shepherds knew Jesus would soon be born. They were happy to hear the news. Wise men also studied and saw the star. They knew that Jesus was born.

Do you like to hear stories from the Bible?

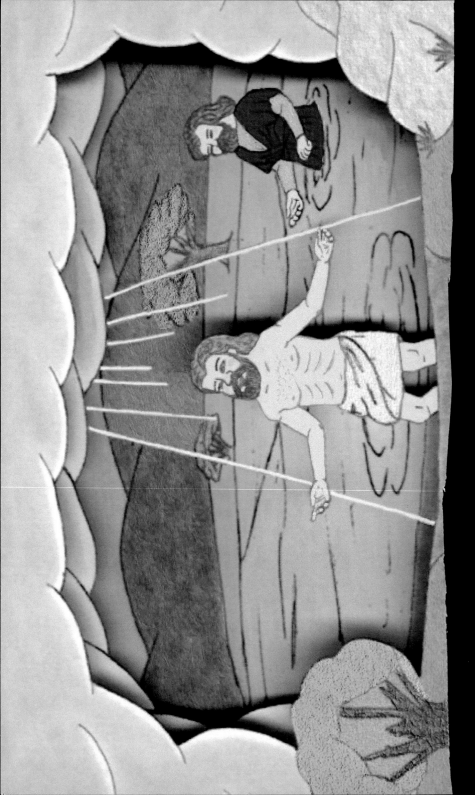

BAPTISM

"Jesus...was baptized of John in the Jordan." ...Then a voice from heaven said, "You are My beloved Son, in whom I am well pleased" (Mark 1:9, 11, NKJV).

Reading the Bible every day tells us what Jesus is like. Baptism shows others we want to be like Jesus.

Have Mommy or Daddy read Bible stories to you. You can become more like Jesus.

9

TEMPTED

"Jesus...was led by the Spirit into the wilderness" (Luke 4:1, NKJV).

Jesus became very hungry. Do you ever get really hungry? Satan tried to get Jesus to do wrong. Jesus said, NO! to Satan.

When you are tempted to do wrong, ask Jesus to help you say, NO! to Satan.

LAST SUPPER

Jesus said, "If I...have washed your feet, you also ought to wash one another's feet" (John 13:14, NKJV).

Jesus washed the disciples' feet. Why? There was no servant to wash their dusty feet.

Do you want to be like Jesus? Be a good helper.

GETHSEMANE

"Father...not my will, but Yours, be done" (Luke 22:42, NKJV).

Jesus wanted to obey His Father.

When we pray Jesus helps us obey, also.

THE CROSS

"For God so loved the world that He gave His only begotten Son, that whoever believes in Him should not perish but have everlasting life" (John 3:16, NKJV).

Jesus Loves you very much!

Do you Love Jesus?

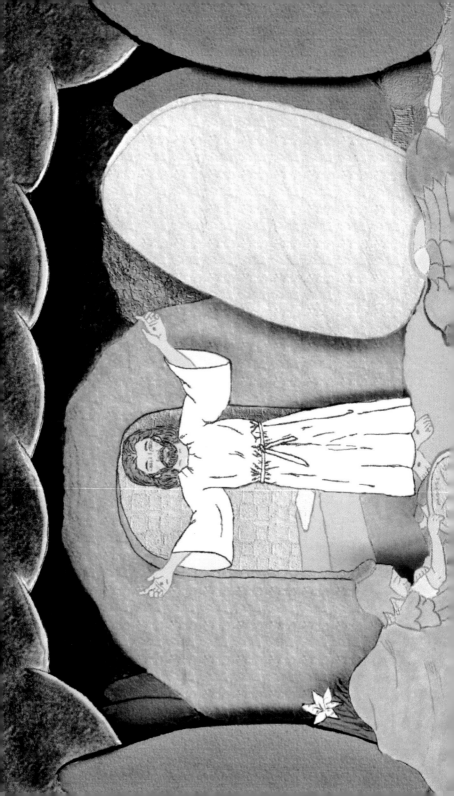

THE RESURRECTION

The angel said, "He is risen!" (Mark 16:6, NKJV).

Jesus came out of the grave early Sunday morning. The guards were very frightened! The priests told them to lie; to tell people His helper took Him away.

Is it right to lie? The Bible says, "Do not lie to one another..." (Colossians 3:9, NKJV).

MARY SEES JESUS FIRST

Jesus said, "Why are you weeping? Whom are you seeking?"
(John 20:15, NKJV).

Mary did not know Jesus at first. But when He said her name she was so happy!

Are you happy when you hear Mommy or Daddy say your name?

21

JESUS ASCENDS

"This same Jesus...will so come in like manner as you saw Him go into heaven" (Acts 1:11, NKJV).

I am so glad Jesus is coming back again. The Bible says so and I believe it!

Do you believe what the Bible says?

JESUS COMING

"I will come again and receive you to Myself; that where I am, there you may be also" (John 14:3, NKJV).

Jesus is coming again just like the Bible says.

Do you believe Jesus is coming again? Would you like to ask Him to help you to get ready?

JESUS IS KNOCKING

"Behold, I stand at the door and knock. If anyone...opens the door, I will come in to him and dine with him, and he with Me" (Revelation 3:20, NKJV).

Jesus wants to live with you all the time. But you have to ask Him to come in.

Do you want Jesus to live with you? Ask Him now. He loves you and is waiting for you to ask.

YOU!

JESUS

LOVES

DO

YOU

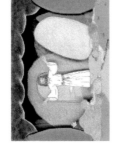

LOVE

JESUS?

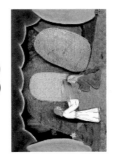

WHAT HAVE YOU LEARNED?

Parents: For the very young, point to each picture and ask, "who is this," or, "what is this," pointing to things in the picture. As they get older, ask the following questions (repetition is their way of learning):

1. Who created the heavens and the earth?
   Jesus
2. Who was born in a barn?
   Baby Jesus
3. Why was Jesus in the water?
   He was baptized
4. Who tempted Jesus?
   Satan
5. What did Jesus do?
   Washed the disciples' feet
6. Who was Jesus praying to?
   His Father in heaven

7. Why did Jesus have to die?
   He loves you and me
8. Did Jesus stay in the grave?
   NO!
9. Who saw Jesus first?
   Mary
10. How did Jesus go to heaven?
    In the clouds
11. How will Jesus come again?
    In clouds with many angels
12. Who is knocking?
    Jesus

We'd love to have you download our catalog of titles we publish at:

www.TEACHServices.com

or write or email us your thoughts, reactions, or criticism about this or any other book we publish at:

TEACH Services, Inc.
254 Donovan Road
Brushton, New York 12916

info@TEACHServices.com

or you may call us at:
518/358-3494